The "C" Book

"C" Words MORE POWERFUL
than cancer, covid-19,
and any life crisis

Robin Waites Tullier

Author Note

Definitions from Webster's Ninth New Collegiate Edition Copyright 1987

Most scriptures used are from New International Version Holman Bible Publishers copyright 1986

Scriptures noted NKJV are from New King James Version

Table of Contents

Preface	ix
CHRIST	1
CROSS	7
COURAGE	11
COMFORT	15
COVENANT	19
COMPLETE	23
CONFIDENT	27
CONFESSION	31
CHAMPION	35
CHARACTER	39
COVER	43
CARE	47
CAN	51

CHOICE	55
CHEER	59
CALM	63
COMMUNITY	67
CREATE	71
CONTINUE	75
CLING	79
COMBAT	83
CLAIM	89
CONSIDER	93
CRADLED	97
CONTENT	101
CLOSENESS	105
COOPERATE	109
CONTROL	115
CHILD	123
COMPASSION	129
CHURCH	133
CONCLUSION	139

Preface

I have been contemplating writing this book for years, and now is the time. The inspiration for this little book of power was born during my late husband's battle with pancreatic cancer in 2006. He was posting a daily blog and started listing and defining "c" words that had more power than the reality of cancer. I have taken his list and added more words to create a resource for those struggling to see hope amid life's trials and struggles. I pray this is an encouragement to those battling this hellish disease or those experiencing a crisis of faith or merely needing a dose of encouragement.

Here are 31 "C" words, a word a day for a month. Each word is followed by its Merriam Webster definition and then explored spiritually to find its more profound, more powerful meaning. So, sit back and grab hold of "c" words that can bring a new perspective to your situation and your soul.

CHRIST

Messiah, Jesus, the ideal truth that comes as a divine manifestation of God to destroy incarnate error

Undoubtedly, this is the most powerful "C" word known to humanity. Despite that fact, many are not aware of the power found in Christ. First, there is the power of Christ to **save**. According to Luke 19:10, *"For the Son of Man came to seek and to save what was lost."* Once we give our lives to Christ, we go from lost to found, from the kingdom of darkness to the kingdom of light. He fills us with

His Holy Spirit, who empowers us to live above our circumstances. Cancer and life crises seem to have the ability to strike fear in the human heart, but Christ said in Luke 12:4-5, *"I tell you, my friends, do not be afraid of those who kill the body and after that can do no more. But I will show you whom you should fear: Fear Him who, after the killing of the body, has power to throw you into hell."* We need to place a reverential fear in God, that He alone deserves. When we do this, the things in life that bring fear come into proper perspective. Although cancer may be able to destroy the body, it cannot remove the promise of eternal life granted to us by our faith in the Lord Jesus Christ. In believing this truth, we can find peace right in the middle of what would bring terror to most people.

Second is the power of Christ to **heal**. Although some people do not receive healing on this side of heaven, it does not change the fact that Christ indeed healed many. All those who came to him experienced healing. The lady with the issue of blood, the blind beggar, the lame man lowered by his friends through the roof, and many more were healed by the power of God.

Healing can come in an instant, or it can progress over time. I have seen and experienced both personally. We will not debate the age-old question about why some people are healed, and some are not in this little book of "C" words. However, I do encourage you to search out the scriptures on healing because healing is for today.

We must realize that healing and deliverance from our situations are not the end game for God; a relationship is. He is more concerned about the condition of our hearts and the relationship He wants to build with us. We can never let the things we want or desire from Him take precedence over just knowing Him. Sitting in His presence and communing with Him far outweighs any temporary fix we receive from Him.

Christ desires a relationship with us, one that is active, vibrant, and very much alive. We need to accept the truth that Jesus is a resurrected man that is alive at this very moment, seated at the right hand of God, the Father. He is not like our deceased loved ones that are currently waiting, as are we, for the resurrection of the dead. Jesus, my dear friends, is ALIVE. He was a person that walked this planet and experienced life in every way as a human, yet He did it without sin. He died a cruel death on a cross, although He had committed no wrong. Our sinless Savior rose again after three days and visited with His disciples. He ate with them, yet He could walk through walls. He showed them His scars. He discussed with them His plans of sending the promised Holy Spirit. He gave them the promise of never leaving them or forsaking them. He issued the Great Commission of sharing the Good

News, and then He was taken up to heaven. This man Jesus is the **CHRIST**; He is the Messiah.

If this is news to you and you have never realized your individual need for a Savior, then you can now prepare your heart for the great exchange. By coming to grips with your sinful nature and realizing that Christ is the only remedy for that condition, you can place your trust in Him and ask Him to forgive you. Repent (turn away) from your sins and ask him to empower you with His Holy Spirit, who will come to live inside of you. Logically, it is hard to understand. However, spiritually, it makes all the sense in the world. Choosing to follow Christ will be the most significant decision of your life and will affect all eternity. Your journey begins now.

CROSS

A structure consisting of an upright with a transverse beam used especially by the ancient Romans for execution

Many may only view the cross as a symbol that depicts Christ's death. But oh, there is so much more that happened on that cross. As we consider the cross and what it means to the believer, we learn about all the benefits gained through Christ's sacrificial act. The cross was a cruel instrument of death, but when Christ was hanging there bloody and dying, it became an instrument used for our redemption. We were on His mind—YOU were on His mind. It was through His death on the cross and His resurrection from the dead that Christ defeated death, hell, and the grave. We are overcomers through Christ's victory and finished work on the cross. It was on the cross that Christ declared, "It is finished." (John 19:30) What was *it* that was finished? *It* was paying the debt that we owed but were powerless to pay. *It* was the reconciling of us to the Father. *It* was securing eternal life for those who believe. *It* was making provision for the abundant life here on earth, as well. Without the cross, there would have been no resurrection. Although you may be frightened and wondering what the future holds, you can be confident that Christ's work on the cross accomplished all you need to victoriously fight this horrible diagnosis or walk confidently through this crisis. There is nothing, I repeat, nothing, that is stronger than Christ and the finished work of **'the cross.'** Hold steadfast to that old rugged cross knowing that your King and Lord, your absolute best friend, went there for you and for the situation you find yourself in right now. As believers, no matter what may come, life or death, you are victorious because Christ took the sting out of death. This truth is also part of His finished work on the cross. That cruel cross became the way by which we gain our freedom.

Place your spiritual eyes upon Christ hanging on the cross. First, realize that He went there and endured that suffering and death for you. Second, recognize that He is no longer there. He has risen, and the debt has been paid. He died on your behalf. Because of that, you are entitled to all that His death and resurrection have bought you. It was finished and is finished, for YOU.

COURAGE

Mental or moral strength to venture, persevere, and withstand danger, fear, or difficulty

When someone is said to have courage or to be courageous, it does not mean they do not experience fear. It is that person's response or behavior in the face of fear that defines them as courageous. Many times, in the face of danger, men and women of God were instructed to fear not, to be strong and of good courage. There is no greater time to hear these words from the Lord than when

you are facing your mortality. The hope
we have in Christ and eternity can allow for courage to grow in our hearts.
Knowing that heaven is our home and
that this temporary existence will be shed
one day for immortality is the true hope
for all humanity. As you go through each
treatment, as you face surgery, or as you
choose to do nothing medically, let courage arise in your heart. Face the giant of
cancer like David faced Goliath. His confidence was not in the weapons of warfare
he was bringing to the fight. His faith was
in the God of Israel. His confidence was
in the One he heard parted the Red Sea,
in the One who rained manna from heav-
en to feed those in the desert. Although
he did not experience these things personally, he knew these stories of old to
be true. They were stories passed down
through the generations. In his personal
experience, he faced a lion and a bear and
was able to defeat them and protect his
sheep because of the strength he found

in God. We read in 1 Samuel 17:37, *"The Lord who delivered me from the paw of the lion and the paw of the bear will deliver me from the hand of this Philistine."* David was able to see the situation he was in with Goliath from the perspective of who God is and was. Knowing the truth about God allowed David to face Goliath courageously and come out victorious.

If you do not know God in this way, ask Him to show you the truth of who He is. Spend time getting to know Him in His fullness. He desires to be known by you. We can search Him out our entire lives, and there will still be more to know about Him. Find your courage in the One who spoke the whole universe into existence. Find your courage in the One who knows the number of hairs on your head. Draw strength and courage from knowing Him and the truth of the promises in His word. Be persuaded, take courage, my dear friend, God Almighty, is on your side.

COMFORT

Consolation in time of trouble or worry

We will explore this word by examining the apostle Paul's words inspired by the Holy Spirit in 2 Corinthians 1:3-4 "... *and the God of all comfort, who comforts us in all our troubles, so that we can comfort those in any trouble with the comfort we ourselves have received from God."* We can have confidence in knowing that first, God will bring us comfort himself, and second, those that God has comforted can also display His comfort. There are certain aspects of God's character that we do not fully understand until we are in circumstances that place a demand on Him to reveal Himself to us in that way. I did not understand this Godly comfort until my husband was faced with his cancer diagnosis. As I purposed to remain in the moments I was in, instead of allowing my thoughts to race ahead to predict all possible outcomes, it was then that I found great comfort in every situation and decision we needed to make. Allowing God Himself to give us comfort is like no comfort offered by this world. It is a matter of getting alone with Him and being brutally honest with yourself and Him. There is nothing you can tell Him he does not already know. However, He desires a relationship with you and for you to speak to Him as you would a friend. This next part is critical. You must then listen. Listen from your heart as he gently and graciously speaks to your situation. Journaling these conversations can be a helpful tool. Allow the Holy Spirit, who is your Comforter, to do His job and bring you into a place of comfort you may have never experienced before.

Receiving comfort from others is also a blessing. Some will send cards and do special things and willingly bring the support that they have experienced from God. These individuals are precious, and God knows who to put around you to help you in your time of need. Keep in mind some people will not know what to say or what to do to deal with the situation you find yourself in; give them grace. Some will say things thinking they are helping but not realizing how their words may be received; give them grace. Some may try to help, but in turn, you may feel they have overreached; give them grace. It is helpful to realize that not all people may be sensitive to your needs or desires, so let them know what you need and desire.

The comfort you obtain from God and others can be like a healing oil that washes over your soul. Learn how to receive this comfort because your heart longs for it and needs it. Let that comfort wrap you tight. Hold on to truth and always look for the light in every situation. The enemy will attempt to paint a dark, gloomy picture; that is what he does. But God knows how to come into your heartaches with vibrant colors and paint the truth. Grab hold of the truth of God's word and the reality of who the Father, Son, and Holy Spirit are. It is this truth alone that can comfort your heart and soul.

COVENANT

A formal, solemn, and binding agreement

A covenant is no small agreement or contract because it is binding, and in days of old, was commonly entered into by shedding blood. Many times, these covenants lasted throughout generations. In the Old Testament, God made several covenants with men. He initiated a covenant with Abraham, promising him that one day he would become a nation of people and his descendants would outnumber the stars in the sky and the sands on the beach. God also made a covenant with Moses and the children of Israel, which is what we, as Christians, consider the old covenant. God instituted this covenant so that humanity would come face to face with its sinfulness and realize their need for a Savior.

God ultimately provided the new covenant with humanity by sending His son Jesus. When a person comes to God with a repentant heart, accepts God's ways by accepting Christ, and becomes born again, he or she enters a covenant with God through Jesus. It was Christ's shed blood and resurrection that sealed this covenant. This covenant is forever. Jesus says in Matthew 26:28, *"This is my blood of the covenant, which is poured out for many for the forgiveness of sins."* This covenant secures our hope of eternal life with Christ. According to Hebrews 9:15, *"For this reason Christ is the mediator of a new covenant, that those who are called may receive the promised eternal inheritance--now that he has died as a ransom to set them free from the sins committed under the first covenant."* But God, in His perfect wisdom, did not stop there. He also sent us His Holy Spirit as a deposit, guaranteeing the truth of all He promised. (Ephesians 1:13-14)

Knowing that a covenant is binding should encourage our hearts. God has no intention of backing out. The agreement that cost Christ His life is not about rules and regulations; it is about faith and relationship. In good times and in excruciatingly tricky times, the covenant stands. There are so many benefits we gain as partakers of this covenant. Abundant life, deliverance, hope, healing, peace, wisdom, eternal perspective, and so much more are just some of the benefits we gain in Christ. Do not let a spoken diagnosis or situation overpower the truth of the covenant that has sealed you in Christ. Stand on the promises provided in God's word, because you are a sure partaker of this divine covenant. Christ's blood does not fail, and He did not make His sacrifice in vain. He is trustworthy, and His ways are right and good. Our circumstances do not get the final word; Christ does.

COMPLETE

Fully carried out

We can find power in the word 'complete' in several ways. First, we know that Christ's work on the cross was and is complete. He said, "It is finished," and there it was - the finished, completed work of Christ. As we live in this completed work, we can have hope in all that that work has gained for us. Jesus left nothing undone. When He said, "It is finished," it was FINISHED!!! Eternal life was made ours, along with freedom, hope, unconditional love, and forgiveness.

Second, we stand COMPLETE. The work Christ has done allows us to stand before the Father justified. When we are justified, it means that when Father God looks at us, He sees the sacrifice of Jesus and does not hold our sins against us. Because we have trusted in Jesus' death and resurrection, we have become new creations. The act of placing our trust in this completed work is what saves us.

Paul said in Philippians 1:6, *"being confident of this that he who began a good work in you will carry it on to completion until the day of Christ Jesus."* We can trust that God can complete the work that he began in us the day we gave our lives to Christ. Daily, as we believe Him, we are undoubtedly becoming more and more like Him.

Knowing that Christ completed the work, the Father sent Him to do should bring us joy and hope. This world is not our home, and Jesus came and completed the task of changing our citizenship. We are simply visitors here looking for a city whose builder and maker is God.

You can fully trust in His completed work and realize that you are completely His. There is nothing that can separate you from this truth. Romans 8:38-39 says, *"For I am convinced that neither death nor life, neither angels nor demons, neither the present nor the future, nor any powers, neither height nor depth, nor anything else in all creation, will be able to separate us from the love of God that is in Christ Jesus our Lord.* Take refuge in knowing that because Christ loves you, He is also committed to completing the work He promised to do in you. This work is an ongoing work of refining and perfecting. It is a work He is well acquainted with performing. He knows what is best for you like the Potter knows what is best for the clay. Yield your life to the Potter's hands; you will not be disappointed.

CONFIDENT

Characterized by assurance

Confidence is what we hold on to in the face of any storm or difficulty. Hebrews 10:35 states, "So *do not throw away your confidence; it will be richly rewarded.*" The truth is our confidence must be in Christ alone. Even as you may be taking treatments of various kinds, you cannot place your trust in medicines, doctors, or surgeries. All those things may help you toward the goal of healing; however, your confidence needs to rest in Christ to use those things to make you well. God can heal in an instant, or He can opt to work through the anointed hands of physicians and nurses. Our Lord is worthy of us placing our confidence in Him. He is a strong and mighty tower, and we can run into Him and be safe. Proverbs 18:10 states, *"The name of the Lord is a strong tower; the righteous run to it and are safe."* There is security in knowing that the Lord of the universe holds us and that He is a friend that sticks closer than a brother.

The enemy's tactic is to disturb your confidence. He will attempt to bring lies to your heart and mind. Of course, he is the father of lies, so this is his usual strategy. His lies will strike at the core of God's identity and your identity as well. He will begin trying to convince you that the promises in God's word are not reliable and surely cannot be trusted. He will undoubtedly attempt to make you believe that you are powerless in the face of your current circumstances. The ultimate end he is working toward is to bring discouragement and doubt.

So, as circumstances and situations ebb and flow, do not let them bring discouragement and doubt to your heart. When things are dark, you must cling even tighter to the truth of who you are in Christ and who He is in you. Allow the Holy Spirit, in you, to assist you in rising above temporary afflictions and grant you a perspective that is from above. Having confidence allows you to square your shoulders and say, "Come what may, I will serve the Lord." Then you can see the bigger picture and realize there is more going on than the obvious. Stand firm, my dear friend, and see the redemption of the Lord. Let the cry of your heart be, "I trust you, God, and I will not be moved."

CONFESSION

1) a disclosure of one's sins in the sacrament of penance, 2) a formal statement of religious beliefs

There are a couple of powerful uses of the word confession. First, it is the avenue by which we gain our salvation. We must confess our sins and believe in Christ's sacrifice to forgive our sins so that we can be saved. According to 1 John 1:9, *"If we confess our sins, He is faithful and just and will forgive us our sins and purify us from all unrighteousness."* Confession of sin is freeing, and it allows us to live our lives in truth and not hide things that God knows anyway.

Also, in James 5:16, *"Therefore confess your sins to each other and pray for each other so that you may be healed." The prayer of a righteous man is powerful and effective."* It is essential to live a life of confession before the Father as well as with one another. Confession of sin keeps the enemy on the run because he knows that confessed sin does not have the power to control us. As critical as the confession of sin is, the need to forgive others that have wronged us is also necessary. We cannot afford to carry around unforgiveness. If we allow unforgiveness to remain unchecked in our lives, in time, it will inevitably lead to bitterness. If we do not deal with this, it can become a killer of our soul and physical bodies. For the sake of your soul and your physical wellbeing, I implore you to find and offer forgiveness to those who have hurt you. Christ made this issue quite clear as He stated in Matthew 6:15, *"But if you do not forgive men their sins, your Father will not forgive your sins."* There is no gray area in that statement, and Christ is not a liar. We must come to understand that forgiveness does not mean we condone or accept the behavior done against us. Forgiveness releases the wrongdoer into the hands of God. By forgiving, we no longer stand as the judge; we allow God to be. How can we accept God's mercy and forgiveness while, on the other hand, give no mercy or forgiveness to others? When we choose to forgive others, we find release as well. In the long run, we enter a place of freedom and realization that God's divine judgment and mercies are far better than ours. Let go of those harbored feelings of resentment; they are only hurting you.

Second, confession is about our declaration of faith. I honestly believe it is vital to speak aloud with our mouths what we believe and to verbalize the promises we are holding close to our hearts. Romans

10:9 states, *"That if you confess with your mouth, "Jesus is Lord," and believe in your heart that God raised Him from the dead, you will be saved."* We are instructed by Paul to speak our confession of faith. Find promises in God's word that you are believing for and confess them. Speak them with your mouth so that not only your ears can hear them but also every spiritual being warring around you. It is crucial in the midst of the battle to offer up confessions of praise with your lips. Let praise and worship become your weapon knowing that God is fighting your battle.

Be mindful of both aspects of confession. Keep a clean slate before the Father, and release others of their failings. Also, declare loudly and proudly, who Christ is, who He is in you, and who you are in Him. As you commit to living a life of speaking forth the Word of God and His promises, you will begin to see things in the natural realm lining up with the truth of God's word.

CHAMPION

A winner of first prize or first place in a competition, one that does battle for another's rights or honor

The word "champion" is synonymous with words like victor, overcomer, and winner. We need to realize that Christ is our champion. He fought for us, and He won the battle. Our hero did not just win an earthly fight over land or rights; He won an eternal struggle for our very souls. He defeated death, hell, and the grave. That is shouting territory. Do we truly understand the depth of that one statement?

We have nothing to fear in death. There is no sting. We do not have to live in fear of hell being our eternal home, and the grave will not hold our bodies down. Our champion, Christ Jesus, died once for all and was resurrected to secure our victory. Now, all we must do is believe this to be true. We need to trust that whether we experience tragedy or triumph, we are winners in Christ. This win/win mindset can set us free. The Word says that it is the truth that makes us free. So, we need to grab hold of the truth about our champion with all we can muster and never let it or Him go.

We need to also view ourselves as champions and overcomers. In 1 John 5:4-5, it says, *"for everyone born of God overcomes the world. This is the victory that has overcome the world, even our faith. Who is it that overcomes the world? Only he who believes that Jesus is the Son of God."*

So, if you believe Jesus is the Son of God, you can overcome this world. The

Spirit that raised Christ from the dead has graciously chosen to take up residence in your mortal body. What? The Holy Spirit, the third person of the trinity, the one who was there at creation along with the Father, and the Son is your abiding comforter, counselor, and friend. If we understood the magnitude of this fact, many of our lives would look completely different. Our conversations would be different, our interactions with others would be different, and indeed, the way we face difficulties would be different. So, own the truth that you are a champion because of the work Christ has done. Life and its situations are no match for the Holy Spirit who lives in you. Wield that sword, the Word of God, with confidence, and know that your champion has already won the war and is also willing to fight your daily battles. Remember, Christ himself said, *"...But take heart! I have overcome the world."* (John 16:33)

CHARACTER

One of the attributes or features that make up and distinguish the individual

Many times, the depth of someone's character can be attributed to the trials they have walked through with God. Throughout scripture, we are encouraged to endure hardship. We are even instructed to be thankful and rejoice in all things, including difficulties. (1 Thessalonians 5:18) How does one survive in the face of tragedy? Genuinely knowing God's character can help us persevere through life's problems. We must remember He is walking through the storm with us. In Romans 5:3-5, we are told, *"Not only so, but we also rejoice in our sufferings, because we know that suffering produces perseverance; perseverance, character; and character, hope. And hope does not disappoint us, because God has poured out his love into our hearts by the Holy Spirit, whom he has given us"*. This scripture is such good news. We can endure because we know that as we walk through trials, God is producing His character in us. Godly character is formed in us while we patiently endure suffering. His character is what people see in us that makes them wonder how we are standing firm in such circumstances. It is supernatural strength that comes only from the Holy Spirit. Sometimes we are not aware of how readily available that power is until we need to draw from it. Circumstances have a way of pressing us into truly standing on what we say we believe. When we let the trials of life have their perfect work in us, only then can we see the fruit of Godly character in our lives.

Also, viewing our afflictions as temporary helps us keep things in perspective. According to 2 Corinthians 4:17, *"For our light and momentary troubles are achieving for us an eternal glory that far outweighs them all.* The Bible says ALL these troubles will pale in comparison to what we will experience in heaven. However, that does not diminish the hurt and pain you may be feeling at this moment. The delicate balance in life comes as we acknowledge the truth of our feelings while also recognizing the lies our emotions try to speak to us. We must be honest with what we are feeling, but always remind ourselves of the truth of God's word.

Allow this time of suffering to produce in you what God intends through this journey. He sees the end from the beginning. As we surrender ourselves to God, the enemy has no dominion, he has no victory, and he must flee. As you keep an eternal perspective, let Christ's character be forged in you. Becoming more like Christ is the ultimate work of the Spirit. Remember, *"...God has chosen to make known among the Gentiles the glorious riches of this mystery, which is Christ in you, the hope of glory."* (Colossians 1:27)

COVER

To afford protection or security to

How awesome that we can run to Christ for cover. Indeed, this is important in times of need, but I would like to suggest we always willingly stay under His covering. This cover is a place of protection for us. As we commit our lives to Him and surrender to His plans, we remain under His protection. It is when we venture off on our own that we step out from that safe place and find ourselves uncovered.

His name, His blood, and His sacrifice

cover us. Because of Christ and His work on the cross, we are found innocent of the sin that makes us guilty. In the universal court where God, the Father, sits as judge, we are found innocent. We are absolved of all wrongdoing because Jesus so willingly sacrificed His life in obedience to the Father. The Bible says in Hebrews 12:2, *"…who for the joy set before Him; He endured the cross"*. In so doing, we became covered. When our Holy heavenly Father looks on us, He sees the blood of Jesus applied to our lives. He sees the blood covering our once raw, exposed sinful nature. He sees our lives hidden in Christ. Being enveloped in that place affords us many blessings. In that place, we are eternally forgiven as we confess our sins. In that place, we can find a peace that defies human logic. In that place, we can overcome all of life's obstacles. Finally, in that place, we can rest secure in the Father's love for us.

If that hidden place is foreign to you,

I encourage you to search it out. You can find it in surrendering your life to Christ and knowing that He has your very heartbeat in His hands. He sees you; he knows you, and He is certainly capable of taking care of you. Rest under His covering in the shadow of His wing. (Psalm 36:7 and Psalm 91:4) There is no safer place.

CARE

Charge; supervision

"*Cast all your anxiety on him because he cares for you.*" (I Peter 5:7) This verse addresses what we can do with anxiety. Christ has a remedy for what is troubling us. It tells us to cast or throw our burdens on Christ Jesus. Before we can do that, we must believe He cares for us. We must come to some understanding of the truth of that scripture. Jesus cares about you and me. Throughout the Gospels, we are told about the care Christ has for us. We see Him calling for the children to come to Him as He cares for them. We witness Him healing lepers and the blind man who was calling out to Him. Jesus even took the time to speak to a woman drawing water from a well. People's lives were forever changed as they encountered Christ. Jesus' entire life was about bringing care to people. He took opportunities to meet the current needs of people as well as being the answer for all humanity throughout eternity.

We must trust that once we have thrown our cares on Him, He will then bring us the peace and comfort we need. He will replace our anxious thoughts with a supernatural calm, according to Philippians 4:6, *"Do not be anxious about anything, but in everything, by prayer and petition, with thanksgiving, present your requests to God. And the peace of God, which transcends all understanding, will guard your hearts and minds in Christ Jesus."*

For many of us, this is not a one-time act. Casting our cares on Christ may happen minute by minute. Our concerns do not burden Christ; He asks for them. He wants to shoulder them for you and with you. Do not forget the Bible says His yoke is easy, and His burden is light. (Matthew 11:30) Once we are yoked up with Christ, then and only then can supernatural things begin to occur. Only then can we sense unexplained peace in the middle of crisis circumstances. Only then can true hope spring up in our hearts.

God the Father, His son Jesus, and the Holy Spirit care for us. Once in the gospels, it was stated that Christ desired to gather Jerusalem like a hen gathers her chicks. That is an excellent picture of the nurturing, caring nature of God. The Lord knows how to take care of us.

Let yourself be taken care of by Christ. Let go of the thoughts that want to invade your peace. Take a deep breath and, with your mouth, say to Jesus, "You can have it all. It is all yours anyway. You can have me. I'm all yours anyway." In that declaration, receive the care and comfort that comes from Christ alone. He will never grow weary of catching your burdens as you cast them His way.

CAN

Be enabled by law, agreement, or custom

This word implies not only the ability to but also the authority to do an action. There are some things we must realize we have the authority to walk in. We need to acknowledge that the physical world does not dictate to the spiritual world. Most assuredly, it is the other way around. I'm sure when the Israelites were backed up to the Red Sea, or the three Hebrew children faced a fiery furnace, or Daniel spent the night with several hungry lions, they had to rely on the truth of Someone more powerful than their circumstances. It is the same with us when we find ourselves facing giants of illness, disappointment, or tragedy. The word "CAN" needs to be put into action, but first, we must know Who we trust and what He can do.

"I can do everything through him who gives me strength." (Philippians 4:13) What does that mean? It means that we need to realize the power that raised Christ from the dead lives in us as believers in Christ. Confidently knowing who we are in Christ, allows us to walk out these CAN statements in our lives. We CAN overcome, we CAN leap over a troop, we CAN have peace, we CAN be content in all situations, we CAN see supernatural things take place in our lives.

This ability is only possible for us because of the authority of Christ in our lives. There is nothing good in us, and no strength, apart from God in us, can produce supernatural fruit. We are, without a doubt, utterly dependent on God. If we do not acknowledge Him as the One who reigns over the circumstances in our lives, we will be tossed back and forth like waves on the ocean. The only way to honestly know our lives are built on a firm foundation is to trust that Christ knows all, sees all and is aware of every minute detail of our lives. This understanding of His sovereignty brings security to our lives. We also acknowledge that God is omnipotent, meaning there is nothing He cannot do.

We can because He can!!!! Which means, beloved, that you CAN!!!

CHOICE

Power of choosing

I believe one of the greatest gifts from God to humanity is the ability and mandate to choose. Our whole life is about making choices. Every day, we decide what to wear, what to eat, what to think. We make choices about what kind of cars we want to drive, and where we would like to live. Our lives are a culmination of many, many choices.

Many of our choices only affect our day to day natural world. However, there are choices we make that can affect our eternity. The decision to accept Christ as our Savior and Lord has eternal ramifications. That one decision allows us to spend eternity in heaven with God the Father, His son Jesus, and His Holy Spirit. We also have the honor of spending eternity with our loved ones who have gone before us who have died knowing Christ as their Savior.

God told the people of Israel, in the Old Testament, through Moses to CHOOSE life. Moses laid out before them all the blessings for serving God and serving Him alone, as well as the curses for them turning their back on God and serving other gods. They were instructed to choose life. I believe we are still given those choices today. We can choose to believe that God is who He said He is. We can choose to serve Him even in the middle of unexplained circumstances. We can choose to let life and faith come from our mouths. Unfortunately, we can also choose to doubt and feel sorry for ourselves. We can choose to become so inwardly focused that we miss incredible opportunities to help others in their pain. We can choose to live our days complaining and hurting, or we can, by faith, choose to let the Holy Spirit empower us to live with hope and joy in our hearts.

Throughout our lives, we are given opportunities to respond to situations and people. How we respond is up to us. Let today be a day of making choices of love, freedom, and joy. Make choices today that will set your earthly life and your heavenly life on the right track. Our decisions here do affect heaven, and one day we will see whether those choices produced wood, hay, stubble, and straw or whether those choices produced gold and precious stones. (1 Corinthians 3:12) Jesus said that we could build up treasures in a heavenly storehouse where moth and vermin do not destroy. (Matthew 6:20) As we go about our lives, we can make choices that lead to deposits in that heavenly storehouse.

You are empowered by the Holy Spirit to make choices, here and now, that can bring about life. The choice is yours. Choose life; choose Christ.

CHEER

To instill with hope or courage.

Several times we are encouraged in the New Testament to be of good cheer. In John 16:33 NKJV, Jesus said, *"These things I have spoken to you, that in Me you may have peace. In the world you will have tribulation; but be of good cheer, I have overcome the world."*

Through Christ, we can be of good cheer and take courage. Knowing Christ overcame the world should bring us great comfort. He overcame temptation; He overcame sickness; He overcame doubt;

He even overcame death. By our strength alone, we cannot find cheer in troubling situations. Only when we surrender our will to Christ can something supernatural happen. We have all probably witnessed people in our lives that have faced adversity with strength and faith. That did not just happen, and it is not merely because of their determined personality. Good cheer is born in our spirits by way of the Holy Spirit being allowed to operate in our lives.

Cheer is also synonymous with joy and happiness. We have also been commanded to rejoice in everything. Philippians 4:4 says, *"Rejoice in the Lord always. I will say it again: Rejoice!"* That is a tall order. How do we rejoice in disheartening things? I believe the only way that is possible is to have a revelation of the truth of who Christ is and what the hope of eternal life is all about. If we remain focused on the temporary and live our lives constrained by what we see, we will find it difficult to even think about being joyful under these challenging situations, much less be joyful in them. But with just one glimpse of truth and one word spoken to our hearts by the Holy Spirit, things can miraculously take on an entirely different perspective. When our view is horizontal, and our eyes are only seeing in the natural, we can become overwhelmed. But when we have a glimpse of heaven and cast our eyes heavenward, now, that changes things. Once we realize the truth that this world is not our home and that we are merely passing through on our way to our actual residence, we can then begin to loose our grip on things and people we love. At that point, we are empowered to place them into God's capable hands.

Heaven is our home; our citizenship is there. We have something to do there, and the Lord has a purpose for us in eternity. We are not just going to sit on clouds, strumming harps. We will be ruling and reigning with him. Ruling and reigning indicate administration and action. I cannot venture a guess of what heaven will look like, but, oh, I am excited about what that opportunity holds for each of us.

So, chin up, and be of good cheer. If your heart is downcast, ask the Lord to fill you with hope and an expectation of what lies ahead. Ask the Holy Spirit to give you an eternal perspective. Take your eyes from looking horizontally and gaze vertically and catch a glimpse of all that truly matters. Catch a glimpse of Him.

CALM

A state of tranquility

In Christ, we can find a calmness that transcends the situations we face. The truth is that we can take refuge in Him. As we abide in Him and He in us, there is a supernatural exchange that takes place. The storms of life will come, but as they do, we can have an abiding calm within us as we navigate our lives through them.

When Christ said, "Peace, be still," to the wind and waves, they obeyed. (Mark 4:39, NKJV) He has the authority and power to calm the storms of life as well.

Even if the difficulties do not cease, we can be calm while we are in the middle of them. The bible instructs us not to be anxious about anything but instead to pray with thanksgiving. As we pray, we receive the peace of God (calm) that passes all understanding. It is a peace that defies explanation. Only Christ can offer this sort of calm (peace). Life consists of one rollercoaster ride after the other, but in Christ, we do not have to white-knuckle the ride. Instead, we can throw our hands in the air and shout out, "I trust you, Jesus."

So, find a quiet place, close your eyes, take a deep breath, and exhale. Ask Jesus to come into the situation and speak peace. Acknowledge your need for Him to calm your thoughts and ask His Holy Spirit to bring to your remembrance all the truths about peace and security in Christ. Tell Him that you are aware of His sweet, abiding presence in your life. As you do these things, you will sense

His closeness. Tell Him everything you feel and think. Let Him know what bothers you, what scares you, and what may even be tormenting you. However, do not forget to tell Him what you are thankful for and how much you love Him. After that, sit back and open yourself up to how much He loves you. Receive, my friend, receive from our precious Savior. He has you, and there is no better place to be.

COMMUNITY

A unified body of individuals

Sharing life with people as part of a community is something special. The body of Christ, which we have the privilege of being a member of, is unique, and we should not take it for granted. It is of utmost importance to find a community of people with whom we can fellowship. I am not talking about just going to church every Sunday and leaving, feeling like you have fulfilled your Sunday obligation. I am talking about people you can be real and vulnerable with; people you can share with honestly and them with you. I am talking about people who will pray with you in times of difficulty and ask you the hard accountability questions when necessary. We need a group of people who will pray alongside us through problems and speak the truth when the enemy is attempting to lie to us in our times of weakness.

When you have found this type of community, there is a blessing there. In Psalm 133, David says, where the brothers live in unity, the Lord bestows His blessing, even life forevermore. After reading this, it stands to reason that community is something particularly important to the Lord. He desires for us to find a community of believers and become actively involved. If we merely go to church to serve an obligation, we are missing a dynamic that is critical to our growth and maturity in the Lord. God never intended for us to walk our Christian walk alone.

Sometimes, we do not realize the

importance of such a community until we find ourselves in great need of encouragement. When you invest time, love, and effort in building relationships, you will receive a blessing from that effort. Having people pray for you, do spiritual warfare on your behalf, and listen to you in difficult times is incredibly important.

We know that Jesus will never leave us or forsake us, and we are never alone, but there is something special about community and having likeminded people walk with us when life gets tough. We are encouraged in Hebrews 10:24-25, *"And let us consider how we may spur one another on toward love and good deeds. Let us not give up meeting together, as some are in the habit of doing, but let us encourage one another—and all the more as you see the Day approaching."* There are strength and power in numbers. Therefore, it is essential to experience life in a community.

You do not choose this group of people because of the cars they drive or the clothes they wear. You need to make this decision based on how real and authentic they are willing to be. Vulnerability should start from the pastor and be part of the culture developed there. If you sense the need to mask your true identity to feel like you belong, that is not the place or people for you. Only when you are comfortable to strip away all pretense and be real with others can you experience lasting relationships and sincere fellowship. I encourage you to seek this out if it is not currently part of your life. It is well worth the effort to find your people. Happy hunting.

CREATE

To bring into existence

In the beginning, God created. He began all things by actually speaking them into existence. Nothing that exists now ever existed before God said, "Let there be." Our God, by His word, made an entire universe. He put stars in their places and decided that human life, created in His image, was going to be His expression of LOVE. As vast as the universe is, God also created the smallest things like atoms and single-celled organisms. He is enormous in scope, yet incredibly intimate and precise in His design. Our Father is aware of all matters concerning us.

Unfortunately, because of the fall in the Garden of Eden, life, which God had intended to be beautiful and eternal, ended. Physical and spiritual death was brought on humanity by the first act of sin. Because of that dreadful act, we have all since been born into a depraved, sinful condition. Not only that, but creation is crying out for redemption as well. We live in a fallen world and are trapped in a fallen state of being. But in God's great sovereignty, he made provision for this falling away: His only Son, the man Jesus. He is fully God and fully, man.

The Father tasked the Son, Jesus, with the ultimate repair job. He had to take on flesh, live our earthly existence, be sinless, and ultimately bear all the wrongdoings of humanity on His body. In paying our debt, it cost Him His life. He willingly gave His life in obedience to His Father. In so doing, He made a way for us to have a restored relationship with Father God. I Peter 3:18, *"For Christ died for sins once for all, the righteous for the unrighteous, to bring you to God. He was put to death in the body but alive by the Spirit"*.

We must realize that as we abide in our Lord and He in us, we have the power of the CREATOR living within. We can speak by faith and expect to see changes in the natural realm. We can create outcomes, inspired by the Holy Spirit, as we govern our thoughts and tongues. Our spoken words are powerful, and they can either be used to complain and express frustration or be used to speak life and express praise.

As co-heirs with Christ, we can choose to create an atmosphere of love and life by way of our attitudes and words. Fill the atmosphere around you with words of life. Join with the Creator. Speak life. Live life. Love life.

CONTINUE

To maintain without interruption

As we persevere in our faith, we continue in what we believe. We must continue to keep our eyes fixed on Jesus and seek out the path He desires us to travel with Him. We must choose to continue to walk the path He has set before us. Remembering that Jesus is on the road with us and is always at work fulfilling His purposes should bring us a sense of security.

To continue means we do not give up. We do not let circumstances sideline us or keep us from finishing the race set before us. Continuing means, we maintain our faith and persevere in believing.

The enemy may throw many things in our direction, but if we stay the course, he will not be successful in his schemes. The thief comes to steal, kill, and destroy, but we are on the side of the One who gives us life abundant. (John 10:10) Our choice to continue establishes in the spirit realm that we will not be moved. Our decision to continue, against all odds, tells those around us that our confidence is in Christ alone, not in anything this world has to offer.

In Colossians 1:22-23 it encourages us to continue: "*But now he has reconciled you by Christ's physical body through death to present you holy in his sight, without blemish and free from accusation, if you continue in your faith established and firm, not moved from the hope held out in the gospel...*" We are urged by Paul to continue in our faith because of the reconciliation given to us by Christ. Continuing is not optional; it is imperative. It is the difference-maker in our walk with Christ. If we throw in the towel and turn our back on our faith, we sabotage the work of the Holy Spirit in our lives. We need to let Him have His perfect work in us. He knows what is best. We declare, "Holy Spirit, we relinquish our need to be in control and surrender to you. It is our choice to continue in our life-giving faith, which You so graciously provided for us to walk in."

CLING

*To have a strong emotional attach-
ment or dependence*

If you are clinging to something, you
are holding fast to it. In times of trials or
tribulations, we must hold fast (cling) to
the truth. We need to continually remind
ourselves of who God is, His character,
and His promises. Jesus said it rains on the
just and the unjust, which means no one
can escape tragedy and disappointment in
our lives. It is all about how we respond
to it and what we believe about it. We
need to allow the difficulties to have their

perfect work in us. Attempting to resist them can simply lengthen the learning process. As we lean into the things we would rather not deal with and keep our hearts and ears open, we begin to hear what the Holy Spirit is speaking to us. As we cling to the truth of God's word, we realize that what He says trumps any circumstance that rears its ugly head.

In our desperation, we must also cling to the truth of who we are in Christ. The Bible tells us that we are seated with Him in heavenly places. (Ephesians 2:6) We cling to truths as if our very lives depend on them because, honestly, they do. We need to remind ourselves of truths like, we are more than conquerors (Romans 8:37), or with Christ, ALL things are possible (Matthew 19:26). While we are clinging to Christ and the truth of His word, faith begins to rise in our hearts, and we become immovable. At that point, we know by experience what it means to stand with a firm foundation beneath our feet. We are not standing on shifting sand. God's word, the truth, is rock solid. (Matthew 7:24-27)

In my mind's eye, I see clinging as if we are hanging on for dear life, like holding on to a lifesaver in a deep ocean. So, let us wrap our arms tight around Jesus, our lifesaver, and cling ever so tightly to His word: His words are life.

It is also comforting to understand that God clings to us as well. In Psalm 139:10, the Bible says, *"even there your hand will guide me, your right hand will hold me fast."* When we are born again (John 3:3), we are placed securely in the Father's hand. Once we are there, the Bible says nothing can remove us from God's hand. (John 10:29) God holds us forever until which time we are standing with Him face to face.

We can cling to God while He clings to us. What better place could we be? Hold on, dear one, the Father has you, and as you hold fast to Him, He will not let you be overcome.

COMBAT

To struggle against

The thought of combat does not usually elicit secure, peaceful feelings. However, we must realize there is an unseen battle raging all around us. Our ignorance of this battle does not change the fact that it is occurring. The enemy of our soul would like us to remain in the dark about this spiritual warfare. The Bible teaches clearly in the New Testament about the war we are in as believers. In 2 Corinthians 10:3-4, it states, *"For though we live in the world, we do not wage war as the world does. The weapons we fight with are not the weapons of the world. On the contrary, they have divine power to demolish strongholds."* We are also told in Ephesians 6 to put on the full armor of God. We do not go into combat with fear; instead, we go armed and empowered with authority. We also go into battle equipped by His Holy Spirit. We battle in the spirit realm from a place of victory because we know Christ has won the war. We also have the power of His shed blood on the cross, not to mention His final act of power—the resurrection. Once we grasp the truth of this victory, our lives will look different from those around us who live with no hope.

Remember, our praise is a weapon. Keeping the sovereignty of God front and center in our praise and acknowledging who He is, allows us to see our situation from a proper perspective. God reigns over all, and He is quite capable of stepping into our mess. Just call on His name. Things around you may or may not change, but **you** will change right in the middle of what you are going through. Ultimately, that is what God wants. He wants us to improve, to be conformed into the image of His dear Son, Jesus.

Also, remember the Word of God is your weapon. According to Ephesians 6, we are instructed to take up the Sword of the Spirit, which is the Word of God. It would benefit us greatly if we committed His Word to memory. In so doing, we will store great power within us. The Holy Spirit will draw from this well of scripture in times of difficulty. The scriptures are not just words on paper. Quite the contrary, our Bibles hold within them the inspired Word of God almighty. Hebrews 4:12 instructs us, *"For the word of God is living and active. Sharper than any double-edged sword, it penetrates even to dividing soul and spirit, joints and marrow; it judges the thoughts and attitudes of the heart."* That verse is most telling. As we become consumers of the Word, God begins doing some powerful things in our lives. Through His word, He can help us discern between the soulish realm (mind, will, and emotions) and the spirit realm. We can then understand things of the flesh versus the spirit. The Word also allows us to judge the thoughts and intentions of our hearts. Being able to make these insightful judgments is helpful as we navigate relationships as well as other things we encounter in life. Once we grasp that the spirit world and the natural world exist and are most certainly in opposition to each other, we then live attuned to the mind of Christ. When we are born again, a great exchange happens. It is our justification. We are instantly made right before the Father. However, at that point, a process also begins. It is the process of sanctification. This process is about walking out the salvation we were freely given. Through sanctification, we are being made into the image of Christ. Dear saints, that process will continue until we stand before Him. Becoming a student of His word is part of that sanctification process and leads us into a life of victory.

Here is a side note. Victory may look altogether different than what we desire it to be. It is our task to fight the good fight of faith and then let Jesus define what success looks like. As Jesus hung on the cross beaten and bloodied, I am sure it seemed as though the enemy had won, and there was no victory in sight. However, three days later, as He rose from the dead, sin and death were defeated, and victory was assured. Remember, in war, that some battles may seem like failures. You must keep front and center in your thoughts that Christ has won the ultimate victory, and the enemy knows full well his destiny. He is just screaming and shouting his way to hell.

CLAIM

To take as the rightful owner

To make a claim is to place a demand. Another part of the definition is "to assert in the face of possible contradiction." When our bodies are sick, or the situation we are in seems dire, speaking the Word of God in those situations may seem contradictory to what we are experiencing. That is where our faith must come in. We must look at circumstances that are contrary to the Word of God and believe otherwise. That does not mean you are in denial; it simply means you have chosen to believe what the Word of God says. Because we believe in the Word of God, we then claim His words to be true.

Once we accept the truth that the eternal realm is more of a reality than the natural realm, we are on to something. 2 Corinthians 4:18 says, *"So we fix our eyes not on what is seen, but on what is unseen. For what is seen is temporary, but what is unseen is eternal."* I am not saying that if you are sick that you need to say, "I am not sick." What I am saying is that if you are sick, you can acknowledge that you are suffering in the natural realm while still believing in the power of Christ to heal. I am not suggesting that you avoid seeking medical help. I think that we can seek medical attention all the while trusting God to heal through the doctors or heal supernaturally. I have seen people healed, and people die that have tried medical care. I have also seen people healed, and people die that have sought no medical care but only trusted God to heal them supernaturally. You must know God; you must listen to the leadership of the Holy Spirit to guide you on your life journey. There should be no condemnation for whichever path you choose. If you are listening for His leadership, He will guide you.

I will never forget one time I told a doctor I was praying for a miracle that did not include him. He so graciously spoke to me, "Robin, sometimes God uses these hands to heal." I was struck at that moment, realizing I had looked down on the call God had placed on his life to serve and bring healing as well. I quickly asked the Lord to forgive me for not seeing His use of doctors also to bring healing. We must position ourselves to stake the claim of healing, no matter how it comes or how it looks. Claiming the truth of God's word is our inheritance, our right as believers, as His children.

If you are sick or in a life struggle, you can claim that God alone is the author and finisher of your life. You can claim that your inheritance is eternal life. So no matter the outcome, you WIN. Your claim can be that in Christ, there is fullness of joy. You can claim that you are more than a conqueror through Christ. Claim that He who has begun a good work in you will be faithful to complete it.

We must believe that God is not a liar. His promises are yes and amen. Where we deceive ourselves is in thinking that we know what is best and expect the answer to look like what we want or demand. It does not work that way. Claim His word and then trust Him with the outcome. I have repeated this concept several times; however, I believe we must come to grips with it to find lasting peace.

CONSIDER

To think of, especially with regard to taking some action

When we "consider," we are looking at situations and circumstances and determining a course of action. As we consider tragedy and crisis in our lives, we must not only look to natural solutions but most certainly spiritual ones as well. God is aware of even a sparrow falling to the ground, so be assured He knows you and sees you at this very moment in time? He is mindful of the things that concern you and is also well equipped to give you answers and a course of action to see you through. God is intimately involved in our lives, or at least He desires to be. If we have only considered God to be some cosmic force we worship on Sundays, who occasionally gives us goosebumps but also at any minute is ready to smite us, then we are not seeing God rightly. Because we may have this inaccurate view of God, we do not see the whole picture of who He is and what our relationship with Him should be. He is our heavenly Father. He has a great love for us, and that love compelled action on His part. He sent His perfect, sinless son Jesus to die for our sins.

He is a personal, engaging God who wants to be involved in our day to day lives. As we make the consideration to accept His sacrifice for our sins and accept Him as our Savior, we must also consider allowing His Lordship over our hearts and minds. Lordship means we hand over the reins of our lives to Him.

As Paul was instructing us about sexual purity in I Corinthians 6:19, he said, *"Do you not know that your body is the temple of the Holy Spirit, who is in you, whom you have received from God? You are not your own; you were bought at a price. Therefore honor God with your body."* We must realize that we no longer belong to ourselves. We are His purchased possession. We belong to Him; therefore, He determines how we live. Embracing Christ as both Lord and Savior bring with it access to abundant life, which we can experience here and now. I am not talking about an abundance of material possessions. I am talking about an abundance of peace, joy, and love.

Do you believe those things are available for you in the middle of your crisis? If you do not, or you are not sure, I am here to tell you they are. I have walked through the valley of my husband's cancer diagnosis, and I know all that Christ offers is available if we will dare to trust Him. Let Him prove His word to be true.

Tell Him you desire to trust Him to guide and direct your life. Get to the edge of the cliff and jump, knowing our Savior and Lord will securely catch you. Dare to pray and think differently than you ever have before.

CRADLED

To support protectively or intimately

In Isaiah 40: 11, we see a beautiful description of how the Lord wants to take care of us. It says, *"He tends his flock like a shepherd: He gathers the lambs in His arms and carries them close to His heart; he gently leads those that have young."* This scripture portrays a picture of protection and affection. He holds us and cradles us close to His heart. In this place, there is complete security. We need to realize our Father knows how to take care of His children. We need to lean into Him and listen to His heartbeat. His love for us is more profound than anything we can reference. His passion for us has cost Him. It was that love that compelled Him to send Jesus to die a cruel death on the cross for our salvation. Knowing the Father's love and receiving it makes us His. Once we are His, He becomes our caretaker.

Being cradled by the Lord is a safe place. Although things around us may be falling apart, we must realize that God has it ALL in control. Nothing speaks safety, like seeing a child wrapped in their mother or father's arms. Well, we, as children of God, have the awesome privilege of letting our Father hold us as well.

Have you ever seen a parent try to hold an inconsolable or restless child? Sometimes they must be held tight until they can relax in their parent's embrace. It is also like that with our heavenly Father. He holds us tight until we are willing to surrender to His embrace without squirming and trying to take matters into our own hands. Surrendering to the Father's embrace is not always easy because we are not comfortable with that type of vulnerability. Also, we may not understand to what degree God is acquainted with our lives. He desires to walk with us intimately and knows full well how to take care of us. Once we settle the truth of these two issues, we can then exhale and relax. God can take care of the things we have entrusted to Him. We need to realize; He may not take care of things in our timing or with our methods. That is where trust comes in. Rest in your heavenly Father's embrace and let Him hold you through this difficult time. There is no safer place to be.

CONTENT

To appease the desires of

It is reassuring to know that we can find contentment in Christ. Just like Paul said in Philippians 4:12-13, *"I know what it is to be in need, and I know what it is to have plenty. I have learned the secret of being content in any and every situation, whether well fed or hungry, whether living in plenty or in want. I can do everything through Him who gives me strength."* Paul said he found the SECRET to being content. The secret is found in knowing that Christ gives us the strength to endure all situations.

However, if we think we can do anything in our own power, that is where we get off track. Once we entertain the thought that we are on our own and left to handle things by ourselves, we are in trouble. When we are convinced that we are not alone in any of life's circumstances, we can then find true contentment. Christ will help us in the middle of any life crisis we are facing. The Holy Spirit is our abiding promise. That means He lives within our mortal bodies, and He is continually reminding us of the truths of Christ.

Like Paul, we can find the place of contentment in Christ. Allowing God to have complete access to our hearts is the key. We must not hold anything back from Him. God knows if you are angry with Him. God knows every area of disappointment in your heart. However, sometimes we do our best to put on a mask even before God. In doing this, the only person we are fooling is ourselves. If we are willing to have an honest conversation with God, He will meet us in the places we have kept hidden and bring healing. Pretending in our relationship with God gets us nowhere. It only makes us appear religious and certainly gains us nothing. It is when we are willing to lay out every disappointment and hurt before God that deep restoration begins. I strongly encourage you to start that dialogue with Him today. He is waiting.

In the quietness of this moment, take time to acknowledge Him. Ask Him to help you find a place of contentment. He will. Once you are grounded in the truth that you are never alone and you are willing to be completely honest, contentment will begin to spring up in your heart. When Jesus said He would never leave you or forsake you, He meant NEVER.

CLOSENESS

Being near in time, space, effect, or degree. Intimate, familiar

Knowing Christ's promise that He would never leave us gives us confidence. (Matt. 28:20) He has assured us of His closeness. The Holy Spirit is abiding with us, living in us. You cannot get any closer than that. According to Proverbs 18:24, *"...but there is a friend who sticks closer than a brother,"* and that friend is Jesus. He does not head out when the going gets tough. It is in those moments that Christ shines through. In desperate times, we need to acknowledge his nearness. We can call on Him to help us when we are in need. In these times, it is a tactic of the enemy to isolate us and make us feel like we are alone. Sometimes we may feel as though no one understands what we are going through. People may attempt to care, but sometimes they seem to say the wrong things. At these times, we must stand on the truth that Jesus is truly as close as us breathing His name. He is literally living within each believer, and we can find peace and comfort in knowing that to be true. As we ask the Holy Spirit to bring comfort, sometimes, it begins by acknowledging His closeness. After all, He is the Comforter.

Be assured that although some people may not be able to understand what you are going through, Jesus can relate to everything. In His humanity, He was tempted in every way as we are. If you have experienced betrayal, you are in good company, so did Jesus. His disciples, who

He poured his life into, all scattered once He was arrested. Peter, who spoke convincingly about his loyalty, denied even knowing Christ. Jesus' betrayal happened with the kiss from a dear friend, and He stood alone before Pilate innocent; yet accused. I think He can understand the place you find yourself. Loneliness and betrayal must take a back seat to the truth of God's word. We submit to God and resist the enemy's lies; we speak the reality that we are not alone. We declare the truth that our God has chosen to be close to us and desires to comfort us in times of despair.

Jesus is with you; He is in you. Honestly, nothing else matters.

COOPERATE

To act or work with another or others

God desires to partner with us in the advancement of His kingdom. This partnership requires cooperation. Once we realize that we are co-operating with the King of kings and the Lord of lords, what can stop us? Our salvation does not come by anything we do; however, the Bible says Christ will judge our actions and our words. We will have to account for how we lived our saved lives. But we also must realize that just because we do the right things does not mean we are in right relationship with God.

To think we could stand before Him one day and hear, "Depart from me, I never KNEW you." That is one sobering statement, especially since, in the prior verses, the person standing before the Lord is spouting off all the THINGS they have done for Him. Matthew 7:22, *"Many will say to me on that day, 'Lord, Lord, did we not prophesy in your name, and in your name drive out demons and perform many miracles?' Then I will tell them plainly, 'I never knew you. Away from me, you evildoers!"* For years I have struggled with this scripture, hoping desperately not to be that person. A friend told me one time that because I struggled with that scripture, I would not find myself in that category. These were people who merely performed duties in service to God without checking with Him, communing with Him, and being led by His Spirit. They are operating on their own, which is why God says, "I never knew you."

However, God desires co-operators,

and He wants to KNOW His co-operators. This word, "knowing," in the Greek
is "ginosko." This word defines a relationship in which there is a deep knowledge
of one another. Some of the words in the
Greek definition are: be sure, be resolved,
understand. This "knowing" is not just an
acquaintance level knowledge of one another; it is a knowledge forged through
time and difficult circumstances, a knowledge that has a deep understanding of
one another. We must cultivate that in
our relationship with God. While we are
in His word and prayer, we must take the
time to listen because He is speaking to
us by His Holy Spirit. Christ said in John
6:63b, *"The words I have spoken to you are
spirit and they are life."*

As we become better acquainted with
the Lord, we also become more sensitive
to Him leading us. In His leading, we can
co-operate with Him in the plans He has
for us as well as the people we encounter. When Peter and John approached

the Gate Beautiful on their way to prayer, they encountered a beggar, who was most assuredly always there, but He got their attention that day. Because the disciples were in tune with the Spirit, that day would be different for the beggar. Peter and John did not have to bind demons, although sometimes that is necessary. They did not have to beg God to heal this lame man. They knew the Father, so they knew what to do. With only a statement, they directed the man, *"Silver and gold I do not have, but what I have I give you. In the name of Jesus Christ of Nazareth, walk."* (Acts 3:6) Then they took this man by the hand, fully expecting him to walk, and He did just that.

Why do we complicate things so much? I believe when we do this, we pride ourselves in trying to perform in "super-spiritual" ways. Instead, we need to be led by the Spirit of God. Our walk with the sovereign Lord is not a performance. It is an ongoing dialogue, a relationship with someone who is always with us. He is not just available during our quiet or devotional times. He does not only operate if the atmosphere is right with music and lights. He desires to be displayed, and we are the ones who have the privilege of displaying Him.

One day I remember asking the Lord to show me someone that needed prayer. I was going to a doctor's appointment, and on the way, I sensed the need to look for someone wearing a red shirt in a wheelchair. I walked into the office, my eyes searching for this person. I did not see anyone in a wheelchair wearing a red shirt. I checked in, was called back, and saw the doctor. As I was leaving, I saw a lady off to my left in a wheelchair wearing a red shirt. I had already passed her before I realized she was the person I had been looking for. I did not want to miss this opportunity to be obedient, so I turned around and approached her and told her that I felt like the Lord wanted me to pray for her. I explained that I had asked Him to show me someone to pray for, and it was her. She was so kind and told me why she was there. I took her hand, and we prayed together. I assure you God taught me a great lesson that day. If we are available, He will direct us. If we allow God into our circumstances, He will make beautiful things happen in the middle of tragedy and crisis. He will make our journey about others. Psalm 32:8, *"I will instruct you and teach you in the way you should go; I will counsel you and watch over you."*

Right in the middle of what may seem unbearable, ask God how He wants to use you. You are not finished here on earth until you open your eyes in eternity. The enemy never wins when you use every moment to glorify God. Ask Him how He wants to use you today. Ask Him to show you people who may be in greater need than you. Cooperate with Him and prepare to be used.

CONTROL

Power or authority to guide or manage

I do not know about you, but this is an area I struggle with the most. When we give our lives to Christ, we relinquish control, or at least we should. That is the whole concept of surrender. We are encouraged to take our hands off and let God lead the way. In Proverbs 3:5-6, we are instructed, *"Trust in the Lord with all your heart and lean not on your own understanding; in all your ways acknowledge him, and he will make your paths straight."* These verses are quoted by many but genuinely lived by few. Let us explore how we can put these verses into practice. I love that these verses cover every aspect of our lives: our hearts, our minds, and our actions.

First, we are to trust Him with all our heart, which many times requires us to let go and not hold on tight to people or things. Our holding on to people is not an indicator of how much we love them. We mistakenly believe that if we worry and fret about those we love, it somehow shows our level of care for them. What a lie this is. We must place the people we love and the things we care about in God's hands. Doing this requires a trust that defies logic. Sometimes it takes us reminding ourselves moment by moment that God is in control. Trust is how we begin this process. Our **hearts** need to be in an attitude of trust before Him.

Second, God tells us about how our understanding can lead us astray. Our

minds, if not renewed, cannot be trusted. We cannot be confident in our ability to understand things. Many of our parents taught us that everything should be logical and well thought out. I am not saying that when we come to Christ, we throw away our reasoning; however, we must not depend solely on our thought processes. Our minds and specifically, our thoughts can betray us. That is why we are instructed in 2 Corinthians 10:5, "We *demolish arguments and every pretension that sets itself up against the knowledge of God, and we take captive every thought to make it obedient to Christ.* This verse needs to be a priority in our lives as we try not to lean on our own understanding.

Last, the scripture says to acknowledge Him in all our ways. Our ways are our **actions**. As we find ourselves in situations, we should acknowledge Christ before we take any steps. If we are involved in things that we cannot acknowledge Christ in, then it is probably time to reevaluate our actions. In Colossians 3:17, it says, *"And whatever you do, whether in word or deed, do it all in the name of the Lord Jesus, giving thanks to God the Father through him.* I would say this scripture pretty much speaks to all our actions. There is no area in our lives where Christ does not want Lordship.

So, God wants it ALL. We need to surrender our hearts, our minds, and our actions to Him. Christ is Savior and Lord and desires to be trusted by us in both ways. He did not just come to grant us salvation. He also came that we would live life here on this planet in a way that brings Him glory and honor. Often, the difficult times in life expose the truth of our character and our commitment to Christ. It is in these times of suffering that God begins perfecting Himself in us. If we, instead, usurp control from God in those situations and work our best plan to shorten the challenging journey, we are most certainly hindering the work of

His Spirit in our lives. We must inhale and fall with abandon into His arms and His control.

Again, I will refer to the analogy of life being like a rollercoaster ride. I would suggest we approach life with the same excitement and anticipation we have as we are waiting in line to ride a rollercoaster. If we have never ridden this coaster before, we have no idea what lies ahead. There could be a slow ascent to a peak, followed by a breathtaking drop to valleys below only then to be whisked upside down in a loop of disorientation. We start up the incline with the thrill of not knowing what to expect. We throw our hands up and abandon ourselves to the ride. Regardless of the unexpected twists and turns of the rollercoaster, most exit the experience with happy smiles and get in line again. Well, we will not have the opportunity to re-ride the ride of **LIFE**. It is a one and done experience. With that in mind, we must make the most of every aspect of the ride we call life.

We also need to come to a place in our lives where we abandon ourselves to the ride designer. He is the One who orchestrates the ups, downs, twists, and turns of the ride. He knows what is best for you. He also knows that as you stop resisting, you will then be able to enjoy the ride despite the unknowns. Those mountaintop experiences, quiet valley times, even the dark night of the soul are all part of LIVING life. God knew that in the mundane 24-hour cycle of life, the day-in and day-out routine would not lend itself to us having to trust Him. Nor would it accomplish the task of creating Christ's character in us. It takes the thrills, despair, joys, and heartaches to make us people of integrity. It also helps when we realize that there is One far greater than us who holds this ride together. Your trust can be in the truth that He is in control, so there is no need to fight against Him or the ride.

So, buckle up, pull down the shoulder harness, take a deep breath with a smile on your face, throw your hands up, and RIDE the RIDE OF YOUR LIFE. In abandoning your life to Him, you will find ultimate freedom.

CHILD

A son or daughter of human parents

We can take confidence in being a child of God. Not only were we born to two earthly parents, but when we became born again, God almighty became our heavenly Father. Many may say that we are all children of God; however, that would be a fallacy. Only those who have entered a relationship with God the Father by way of Christ Jesus, His son, can call themselves children of God. John 1:12-13 says, *"Yet to all who received him, to those who believed in his name, he gave* the right to become children of God- children born not of natural descent, nor of human decision or a husband's will, but born of God." We are not all just born children of God. We become His child once we have embarked on a relationship with Him as our heavenly Father, through the sacrifice of His Son Jesus.

Knowing that we are his children helps to put everything in its proper perspective. We have become heirs of a great promise. We are not merely servants in a vast heavenly kingdom, but we are joint-heirs with Christ. Romans 8:14-17 says, "...because those who are led by the Spirit of God are sons of God. For you did not receive a spirit that makes you a slave again to fear, but you received the Spirit of sonship. And by him we cry, "Abba, Father." The Spirit himself testifies with our spirit that we are God's children. Now if we are children, then we are heirs—heirs of God and co-heirs with Christ, if indeed we share in his sufferings in order that we may also share *in his glory."* That, dear saints, is the best news yet. We can take this "C" word to the bank. God has called us His children. Since we are His children, we have all the rights of being His child. We inherit eternal life, Christ's righteousness, abundant life, and all the fruits of the Spirit and His gifts. If you are unaware of these fruits and gifts, take time to familiarize yourself with them because they are yours to possess. Do not live your earthly life with less than what the Holy Spirit has provided for you. The enemy of your soul wants you to stay ignorant of what has been provided for you so that you will live a powerless life. Do not let that happen. Dig in, read the scriptures, and partake of your Godly inheritance. Start living the abundant life now. The abundant life Jesus promised does not start when you get to heaven; it begins now.

The enemy has kept us ignorant of many things and, in so doing, has stifled us, God's children, from the fullness He

∽ 125 ∾

has provided. One of the biggest lies he tells pertains to our identity. If he can convince you that you are not a child of God and, in turn, make you think that the promises of God are not for you, then he has succeeded. It is as if you are born into royalty, yet you are living like a pauper. It would help if you came to realize who your Father is. Once you embrace the truth of who you are in Christ, your life will begin to reflect your new identity. Your attitude will change, your perspective will change, and most importantly, your heart will change. We cannot take for granted the sonship we have in Christ. He paid the ultimate price for our relationship to be made right with the Father. If we settle for anything less in our lives, we cheapen Christ's generous sacrifice.

Do not let the enemy continue to rob your identity. Begin declaring who you are in Christ and who He is in you. Let the enemy know that you know who you are and whose you are. Live with an ever-increasing understanding of your inheritance in the Father. As you begin to wrap your mind around the truth of who you are, things in life will take on new meaning. The enemy of your soul will no longer be able to rob you of your great reward, your inheritance. Look in the mirror and be convinced of who you belong to and who you are.

COMPASSION

Sympathetic consciousness of others' distresses together with a desire to alleviate it

We can find comfort in knowing that our heavenly Father is the Father of compassion. We see in 2 Corinthians 1:3, *"Praise be to the God and Father of our Lord Jesus Christ, the Father of compassion and the God of all comfort."* Compassion is not just a feeling of sorrow for someone. Compassion is rooted in a heartfelt desire not only to be aware of someone's problems but also to do something to bring comfort in the situation.

Christ has the characteristic of compassion. He desires to show His kindness to us. Remember when we spoke of Christ wanting to gather Jerusalem as a hen gathers her chicks. What brought Christ such sadness was their unwillingness to be gathered in by Him. We need to come to a place of willingness and allow the Lord to gather us into a secure place in Him, a place of refuge. Regardless of what is happening in our lives, being hidden in Christ is our place of safety. In scripture, He is described as our high tower, our refuge, our cleft in the rock. When tragedy and disappointment come, and they will, we can run to our compassionate Father by way of His son Jesus Christ. He does not lack compassion for us. Knowing this can be the difference-maker as we walk out difficult times in our lives. We have a compassionate Father.

Another aspect of compassion is the compassion we gain for others and from

others as we walk through trials. Once
we have encountered troubling times in
life, we are then able to be compassionate toward those in similar situations.
There is nothing like realizing that we are
not alone in our struggles. When we understand that others have walked similar
paths, it can bring comfort to our hearts.
When someone offers compassion from
a place of knowing, it comes with much
more sincerity because they have been
where we are. We are then able to pro-
vide that compassion to others. Many
times, Christ's compassion comes to us
through others.

Allow the situation you are currently walking through to become a training
ground for bringing compassion to others. Ask the Lord to show you the bigger
picture. Ask Him to help you lift your gaze
from the discouragement around you and
place your eyes steadfastly on His face.
Look for opportunities to bless and min-
ister right in the middle of the crisis. As

you do this, you will see the enemy dis-
armed, and you will be able to accomplish
eternal kingdom purposes. Be blessed as
you look beyond yourself to the needs of
others motivated by compassion.

CHURCH

The whole body of Christians

Many associate the word "church" with a building that Christians attend for service. However, the power found in the "C" word church comes when we apply the above definition. The "church" is the body of Christ. The "church" is a powerful dynamic collective. This collective includes believers of many denominations that agree that Jesus is the Christ. We believe that He is the only way to the Father (John 14:6). Together, we trust that Christ is also our soon and coming

King (1 Thessalonians 4:16). We, as the "church," the Body of Christ, are to represent Him, the Messiah, in all His fullness to a lost and dying world. We are an extension of Christ's hands and feet. We are also to be about our Father's business.

It is essential to realize that as the Body of Christ, we are to operate in cooperation with one another. In the second half of 1 Corinthians 12, Paul explains in detail how the different parts of the body are knit together. We are all distinct from each other yet have a beautiful role to play together in the body. It is critically important for us not to compare ourselves to one another and to embrace our individuality in Christ. We each have our strengths, weaknesses, personalities, and temperaments. Although our characteristics should be renewed, we are not robots made to all act alike. We are to accept our differences and be busy doing the work of the kingdom.

As we gather in actual church

buildings, we come together to worship and be equipped. The Lord desires His church to be taught, to grow, and to operate on this planet powerfully. We are to bring the good news of the Gospel to all those who need to hear. We are to display God's love, kindness, holiness, and more. We should be actively engaged in praying for the sick, providing for the needy, and loving those that are lost.

If we examine Christ's life, we see that He ate with tax collectors and sinners, and the religious were offended by Him. Let us be careful, as the church, not to allow a religious spirit to cloud the vision of how our lives are supposed to look. We should desire our lives to look like Christ's. Our daily pursuit is to be conformed to the image of Christ (Romans 8:29).

As we travel through life's struggles, we again look to Jesus as our example. We look at Him, sweating drops of blood as He asked the Father for the cup to be taken away. But as we read further, we see Him bend His will and desire to the will of the Father. What a powerful representation of Christ being fully man and fully God. He struggled, as we all would, to accept what was coming. However, He knew that the joy set before Him was worth the journey. With that knowledge, He accepted the will of the Father. We also must walk in complete surrender to God's will. We do not know what is ahead for us from day to day, but we find comfort in knowing that our Lord is in control, and He can be found even in the middle of turmoil.

Rest in knowing that as a member of the church, you are joined with Him. Be confident that Jesus has walked the human experience and is keenly aware of your struggles. Keep your eyes fixed on the author and finisher of your faith. Stay joined to the church, the Body of Christ, because we were not meant to live this life without fellowship and connection with those that are like-minded.

In the community of believers, you will find those who will pray when you cannot muster even a word. You will find those that have walked where you are and can hopefully bring you some comfort. You will find those whose faith is active, and you can draw strength from fellow believers when your faith is weak. Stay connected, child of God, and do not isolate yourself at your most significant time of need.

CONCLUSION

How ironic that the word "conclusion" is also a "c" word.

Sometimes I wonder if we fully grasp the extent of what happened when Christ rose from the dead. Many celebrate His resurrection as just a holiday in the spring and take it is a matter of fact. Let us shake ourselves awake!!! This event changed the course of history and determined the outcome for all eternity.

Just suppose that you witnessed the death of someone you love dearly, you had a service for them, and you saw them buried. Imagine going to visit their gravesite only to find that they had RISEN from the dead. Would you not be ecstatic, would you keep the miracle and excitement to yourself? But this was not just any person. Jesus was and is and is to come, the Son of God.

However, daily we live with this truth inside of us. We speak not a word to those around us. We neglect to tell of the risen Savior and the truth about His power to save, heal, and restore.

In the song "Christ is Risen" by Matt Maher, there is a line that says— "He defeated death by death." What a profound statement. To be victorious over death, Christ had first to submit Himself to death. The only way to show death who was boss was for Him first to die then rise from the dead in the fullness of life eternal. Our ultimate victory in this life is KNOWING that when we close our eyes at the end and our earth-suit malfunctions, we are still alive in a realm and dimension of the Spirit we have yet to fully comprehend. Do you get it? You never die; you just shed the earth-suit you were given to engage this earthly existence. Your temporary, earthly life gives way to eternal life.

I have come to understand that to walk in the fullness of this life; we must embrace the truth about death. It is not a loss but gain (Phil. 1:21), it is not defeat but victory (I Cor. 15:55-57), and it is not sorrow but joy (Matt 25:21) NKJV. Realizing these truths about death brings freedom and makes us dangerous to the kingdom of darkness. That is why the verse in Revelation 12:11 says, *"They overcame him by the blood of the Lamb and by the word of their testimony; THEY DID NOT LOVE THEIR LIVES SO MUCH AS TO SHRINK FROM DEATH."* (emphasis added) The only way we can do this is to believe and know that this life is simply a shadow, and authentic living begins at the point of our earthly departure. Join me in living with the confidence that, IN CHRIST, we have victory in ALL things, even victory over DEATH.

God has plans for you which include marvelous experiences despite the challenging situations you may have to walk through. You can enjoy life in its fullness when you conclude that at the end of it all, He is going to be worth it. There is nothing life can throw your way that will compare to what eternity with Him will be. You must keep a heavenly perspective and not be dragged down by the temporary trials that loom so large in your mind. Remember that no matter what, with Christ, YOU WIN!!!!

CPSIA information can be obtained
at www.ICGtesting.com
Printed in the USA
JSHW031047251020
9038JS00004B/11

9 781977 230232